THE FRANK ZAPPA GUITAR BOOK

Copyright © 1982 Munchkin Music
7720 Sunset Boulevard, Los Angeles, CA 90046
All Rights Reserved. Made in USA.

ISBN 978-1-4950-6489-0

7777 W. BLUEMOUND RD. P.O. BOX 13819 MILWAUKEE, WI 53213

Visit Hal Leonard Online at
www.halleonard.com

THE CON- TENTS

Introduction 4
Steve Vai, Transcriber 6
The Copyists 7
Notation 8

Shut Up 'n Play Yer Guitar 9
five-five-FIVE 10
Hog Heaven 17
Shut Up 'n Play Yer Guitar 23
While You Were Out 44
Treacherous Cretins 70
Heavy Duty Judy 79
Soup 'n Old Clothes 90

Shut Up 'n Play Yer Guitar Some More 107
Variations on The Carlos Santana Secret
    Chord Progression 108
Gee, I Like Your Pants 118
The Deathless Horsie 124
Shut Up 'n Play Yer Guitar Some More 136
Pink Napkins 153

**Return Of The Son of Shut Up 'n Play
    Yer Guitar 159**
Stucco Homes 160

You Are What You Is 205
Theme from the 3rd movement of Sinister
    Footwear 206

Joe's Garage, Acts II & III 213
Watermelon in Easter Hay 214
Packard Goose 226
Outside Now 243
He Used To Cut The Grass 250

Sheik Yerbouti 269
Sheik Yerbouti Tango 270
Rat Tomago 275
*Mo' Mama 281

Zoot Allures 291
Black Napkins 292

**A Few Words For Those Who Managed To
    Get This Far 302**

*unreleased selection

INTRO-DUC-TION

by Steve Vai

The works in this book were transcribed between January, 1979, and August, 1981-whenever I wasn't touring with Frank.

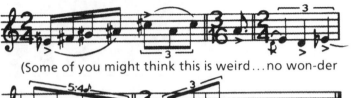

(Some of you might think this is weird...no won-der ...It's not ex-act-ly nor-mal, but what the hey.)*

The songs were first taken off the albums and put onto cassettes. The songs from *Joe's Garage* were transcribed off a small Sony tape machine. The stuff from the guitar albums were bounced to a four-track tape deck, and some were done at half speed.

The guitar solos from *Joe's Garage* (except "Watermelon In Easter Hay") were solo tracks that were taken from different live concerts through the years and printed on studio rhythm tracks. The rest are live recordings from the *Shut Up 'n Play Your Guitar* albums and others.

If you're into this kind of reading it might be a good idea to study them piece by piece. This may encourage you to transcribe on your own which is good for your ears, reading, soloing, and psychiatrist. It may be a good idea to start on a simpler tune. Let's face it, this isn't "Sight Reading 1."

Some of the rhythmic notation may seem ambiguous. On a few licks, where there are several ways to write them, I chose the way which accents the phrasing.

The "Theme from the Third Movement of Sinister Footwear" (formerly titled "Persona Non Grata") appears on the album *You Are What You Is*. On that track Frank's guitar line was doubled by electric guitar, percussion, and bass clarinet. The original rhythm track was replaced by what you hear on the album.

Looking at this book some 37 years after I started the transcription process reminds me of that period in my life when virtually all things were Frank. I'm constantly asked what it was like to work for him and what he was like. It's impossible to quantify an answer because every day of my life since I've reflected on those days and what I learned by being just a tiny satellite in Frank's vast universe for the five or so years I worked for him. Even today, I never fail to see the potent impact that the school of Zappa had on my career and personal life.

Frank Zappa was a highly-inspired person. He was extraordinary in a multitude of ways, but one of his most fundamental gifts was his powerful ability to see a musician's unique potential, perhaps clearer than the musician could. He would then cultivate their exceptional creative oddities and use them in his music. He would offer a platform to express the player's inimitable idiosyncrasies, but always under his selective discretion. Frank was always striving to find extremes and the player was more than willing and excited to go there with him.

I had started transcribing music in grade school, but it wasn't until I started transcribing for Frank that I was offered an opportunity to see where my transcriptional extremes could go. Transcribing his music back in the day was deeply creative and satisfying for me, as it offered me an opportunity to be intimate with my artistic musical instincts. At times I would transcribe for up to 10 hours a day in

* from "Jazz Discharge Party Hats" by Frank Zappa

a state of deep listening meditation. This allowed me to venture into some uncharted rhythmic notational complexities, and it was Frank that recognized and encouraged this ability in me. He also offered this opportunity to the copyists of this book, who delivered in an unprecedented way.

Our ability to imagine creatively is unlimited. We are always on the leading edge of creation. The expansion of our imagination is based on our ability to focus on things that come into our awareness that feel like new creative thoughts. These things are presented to us as events in our life, insights, something someone might say, something we may read that resonates on a creative level, etc.

Although some of the rhythmic notations presented in this book may seem deeply complex, mathematical, obtuse and even abstract or absurd, they can introduce to you the concept of a rhythmic freedom that you may not have been aware of before. This is good news for a composer that finds notational rhythmic enlightenment through some of the examples in this book. The book can act as one of those elements that has come into your awareness that aids in the freedom and expansion of your own creative imagination.

The moment that opened up the floodgates to the potential of unique rhythmic notation was when I first heard and saw the written music of Frank's "The Black Page" (both parts 1 & 2) when I was about 17 years old. That piece of music is a historical monolith in the pantheons of unique rhythmic ideas. In the realms of polyrhythmic composition it's akin to the discovery of electricity, and is the core inspiration that led me to the insights that resulted in much of the complex examples in this book. Let's not forget that Frank played it all on the guitar in real time, in his "now" at that moment.

I'm thrilled to see the reissuing of this book. It's a small peek into the incredible creative expanses that Frank was constantly hunting down. Frank Zappa was an explosion of freedom and his contribution to not only the evolution of contemporary music, but also to our social awareness of freedom and expansion, is historical and incalculable. He was truly exceptional.

Best of luck to the musicians who appreciate and can benefit from these publishings. Just don't hurt yourself.

Steve Vai
Jan 1, 2017 1pm
Los Angeles

STEVE TRAN-SCRIBER VAI

Steve Vai (who was six years old on 6/6/66) grew up on Long Island. He went to school in Carle Place, New York, and studied with William Westcott. He studied guitar with Joe Satriani, and, while in high school was a member of various rock bands, including Rayge. Later he attended the Berklee School of Music in Boston. While there, he sent Frank transcriptions of "The Black Page" and "Black Napkins," and a tape of his playing. He then moved to California and joined the Frank Zappa Band in 1979. His duties included playing impossible guitar parts and more transcribing.

Besides playing and transcribing, Steve enjoys producing when he gets a chance. But when asked why would somebody want to write down this stuff, he replied, "…it's probably a mental deformity from birth." Steve grieves with people who try to play this stuff, "I'm not the only two, I used to cut the grass, you know, you know?"

THE COPY-ISTS

The music in this book was hand copied. This process of "Musical Calligraphy" requires a unique blend of musical talent and drafting ability. It is done with many different pens, various templates, and much patience. The four musicians listed here all copied some of the music in *The Frank Zappa Guitar Book*.

David Ocker has copied and orchestrated various music for Frank Zappa since 1977. He also performed clarinet and bass clarinet on Frank's *Sheik Yerbouti* and *You Are What You Is* albums, and the solo clarinet part in the first movement of "Mo 'n Herb's Vacation" was written for him. Also a composer, Ocker is a founding member of the Independent Composers Association, a co-operative presenting organization for new music.

Richard Emmet has accepted the increasing loss of eyesight and hearing as the price accompanying the awesome responsibility for copying and transcribing the music of Frank Zappa, for whom he has worked since 1978. In real life, Mr. Emmet is a composer (and a closet mystic).

Arthur Jarvinen holds a Bachelor of Music in applied percussion (Ohio University) and a Master of Fine Arts in percussion and composition (California Institute of the Arts). His compositions for solo instruments and various small ensembles are heard often in the Los Angeles area. He performs most frequently with The Antenna Repairmen, a percussion/intermedia trio. He also gives solo performances of his physical poetry.

Lee Scott was born in Atlanta, Georgia in 1956. He received a Bachelor of Fine Arts degree in composition from the University of Georgia and a Master of Fine Arts from the California Institute of the Arts. He now works on numerous electronic music projects.

Excerpt from "Packard Goose"

NOTATION

GUITARS:

1. **⌐**   Semi muted, distorted by pick or palm.

2.   Bright, sharp.

3.   Harmonic (fret indicated) or feedback (indicated).

4.   Pinched note (half-harmonic).

5.   Scratch across dead string.

6. **⊕**   Strum with pick slanted to bring out overtones.

7. **(↓↑)**   Rub right hand on neck, causing squeak.

8. **M**   Over a note: mute with palm of right hand.

    M̸   Half muted (mute, then let ring).

9.   Glissando.

10.   Bend.

11.   Quarter-tone sharp.

    Three quarter-tone sharp.

    Quarter-tone flat.

12. **>**   Accent.

    ∧   Staccato.

    ∧   Very short, percussive.

13.   Indeterminate noise.

DRUMS:

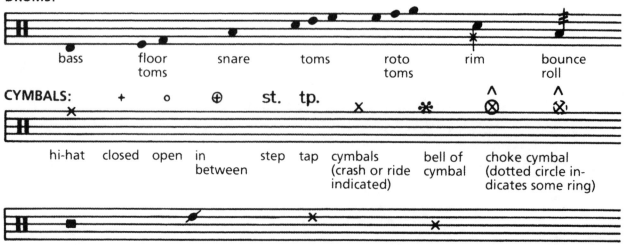

bass   floor toms   snare   toms   roto toms   rim   bounce roll

CYMBALS: +   o   ⊕   st.   tp.   x   ✳   ⊗   ⊗

hi-hat   closed   open   in between   step   tap   cymbals (crash or ride indicated)   bell of cymbal   choke cymbal (dotted circle indicates some ring)

woodblock   castanets   cowbell   collision of sticks   bass drum (huge, tuned to low D)

SHUT UP'N PLAY YER GUITAR

five-five-FIVE   10
Hog Heaven   17
Shut Up 'n Play Yer Guitar   23
While You Were Out   44
    Vinny Colaiuta, drums
    Warren Cucurullo, rhythm guitar
Treacherous Cretins   70
Heavy Duty Judy   79
Soup 'n Old Clothes   90

five-five-FIVE

Transcribed by
Steve Vai

by Frank Zappa

HOG HEAVEN

Transcribed by
Steve Vai

by Frank Zappa

SHUT UP 'n PLAY YER GUITAR

Transcribed by
Steve Vai

by Frank Zappa

gradual modulation to A Dorian (tonic)

Lead & Rhythm Guitars
and Drum Set

Guitars: tune E strings
to low D.

WHILE YOU WERE OUT

by Frank Zappa

Transcribed by
Steve Vai

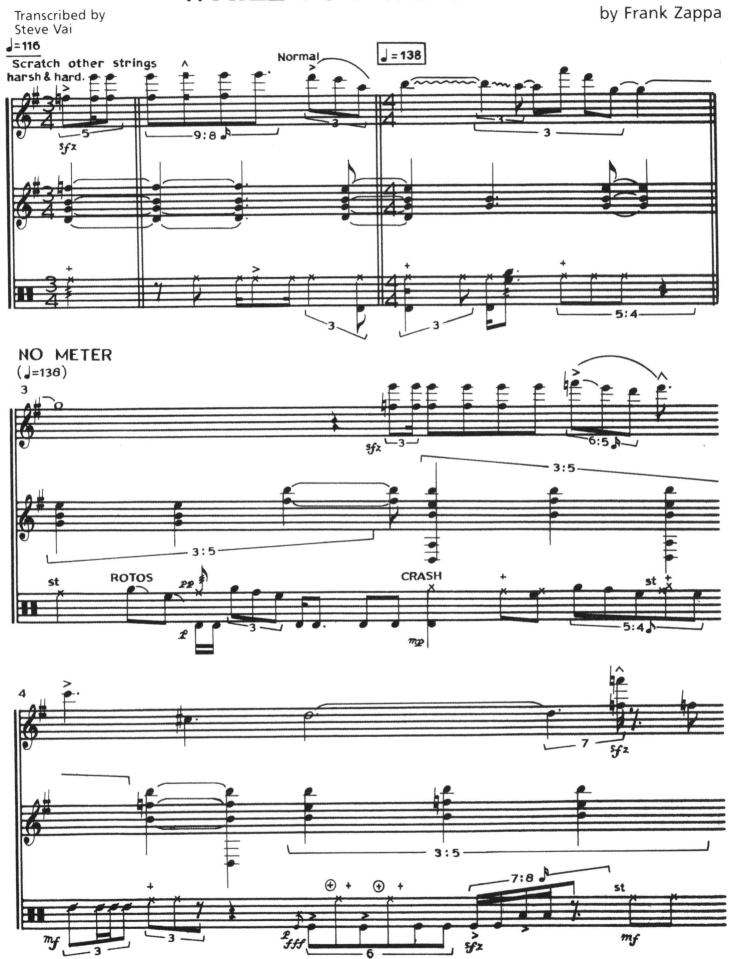

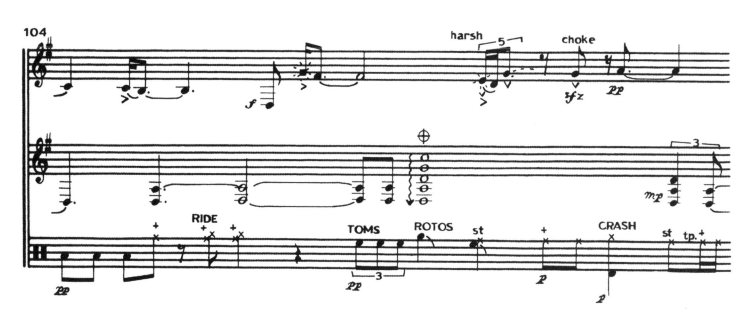

TREACHEROUS CRETINS

Transcribed by
Steve Vai

by Frank Zappa

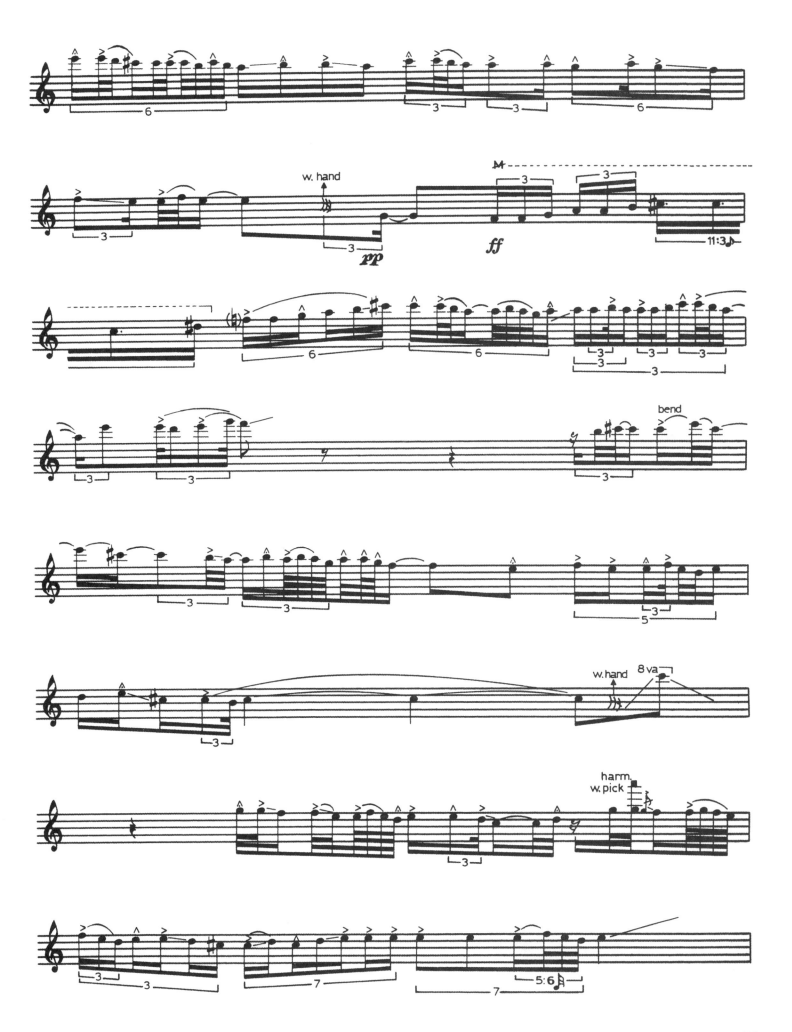

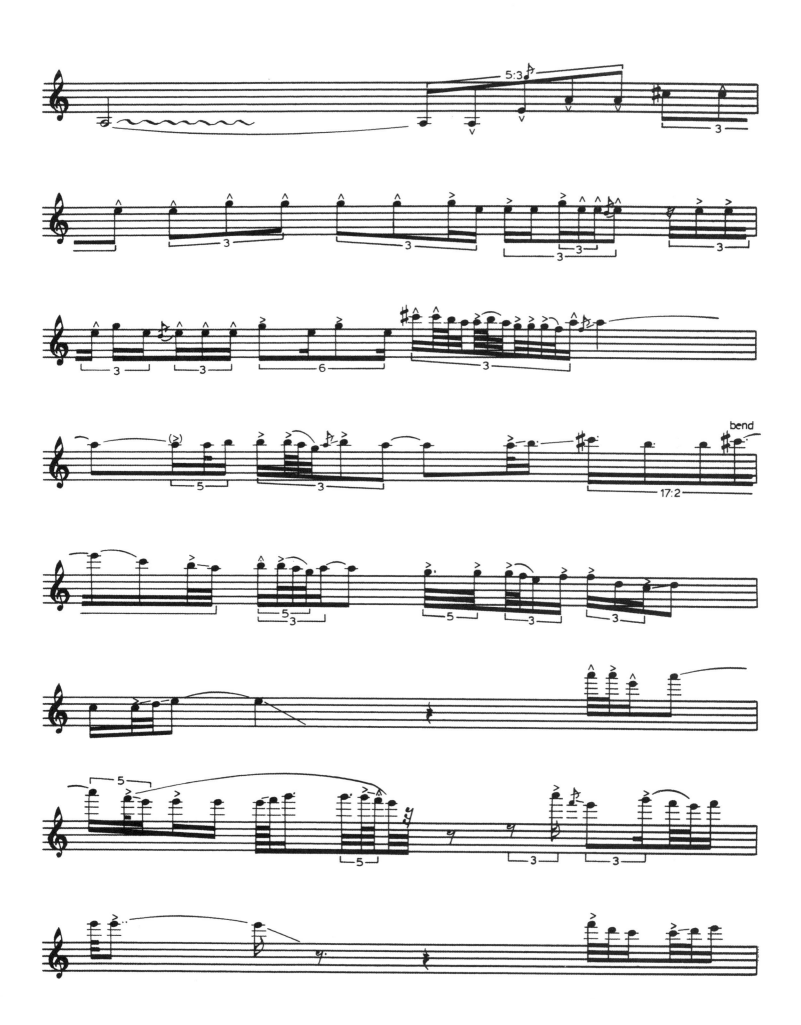

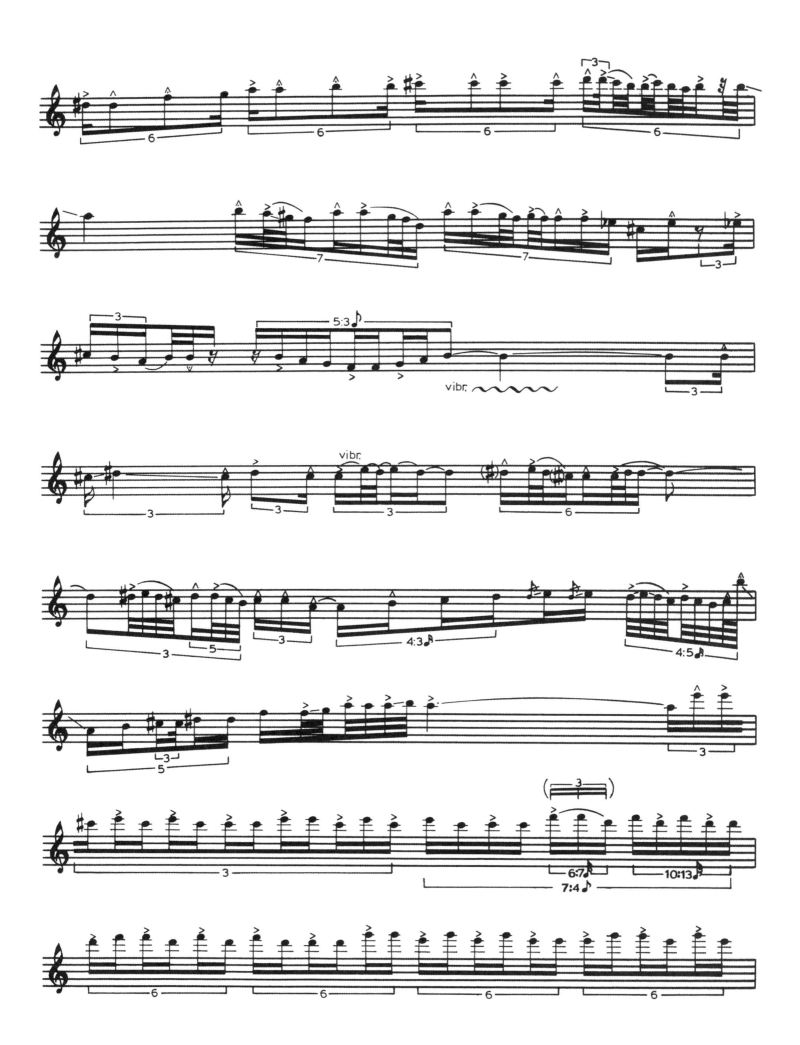

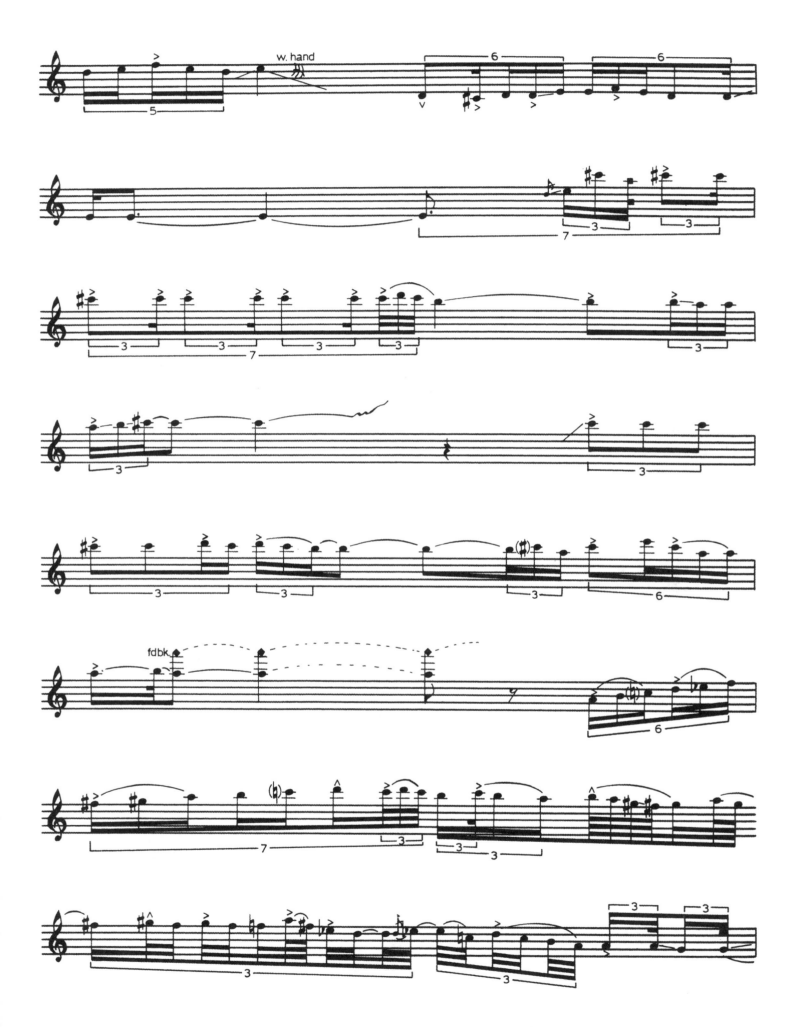

HEAVY DUTY JUDY

Transcribed by
Steve Vai

by Frank Zappa

80

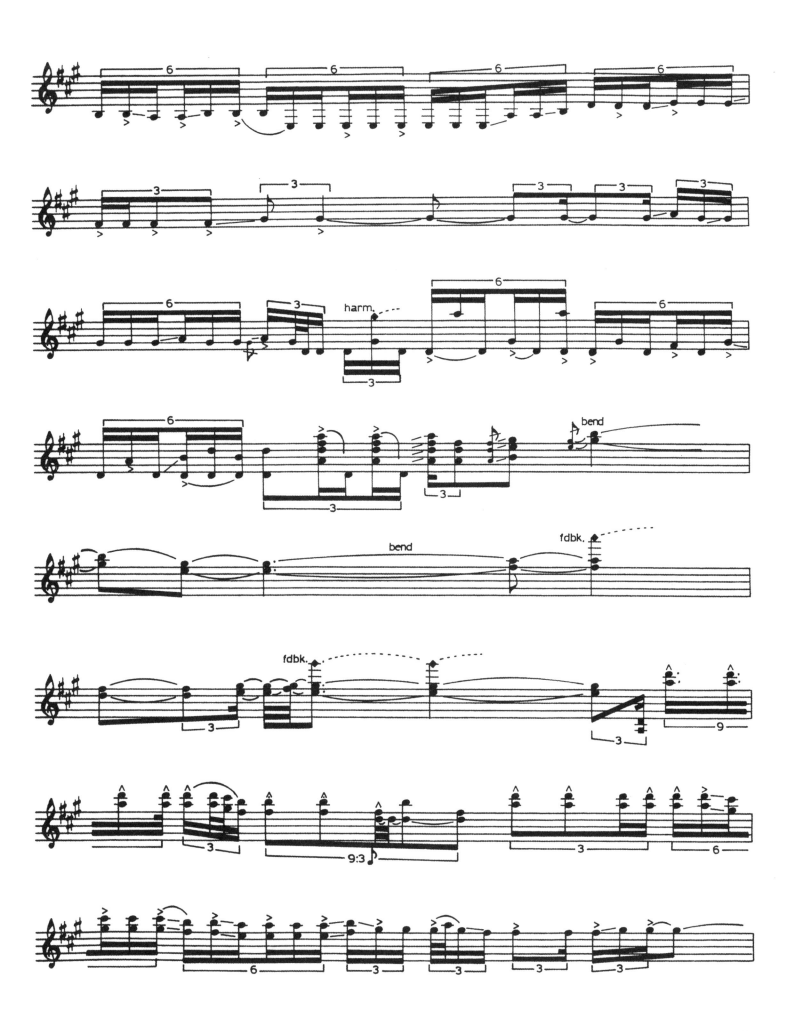

SOUP 'n OLD CLOTHES

Transcribed by
Steve Vai

by Frank Zappa

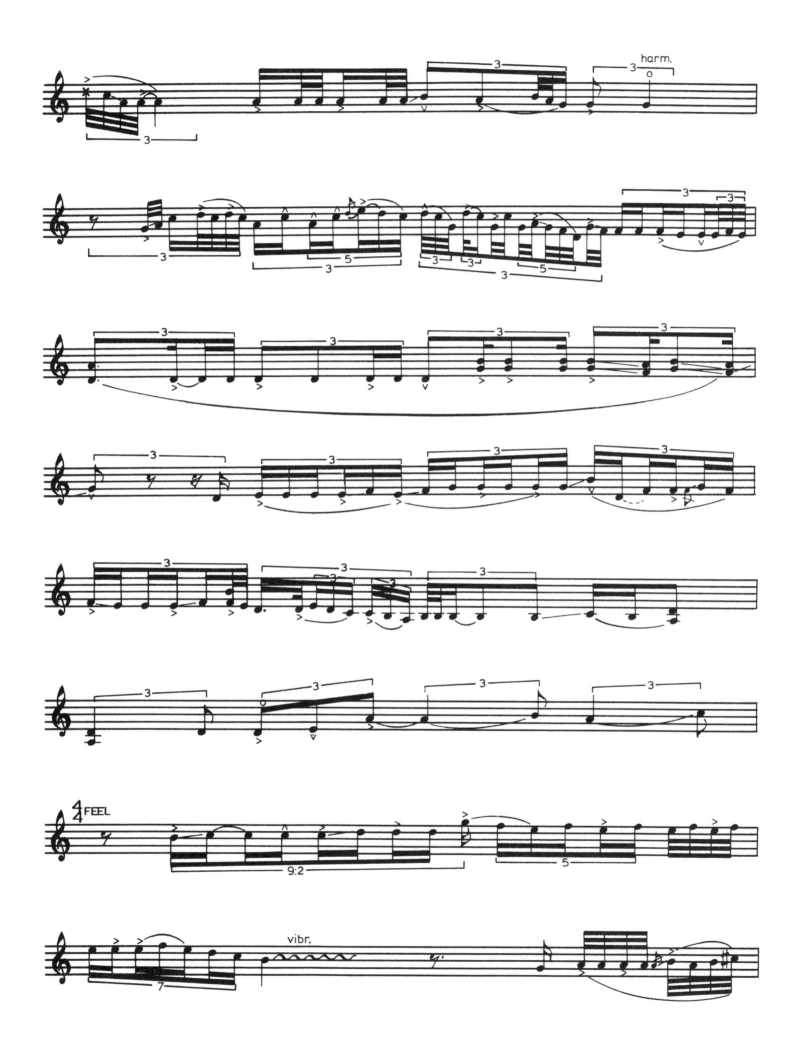

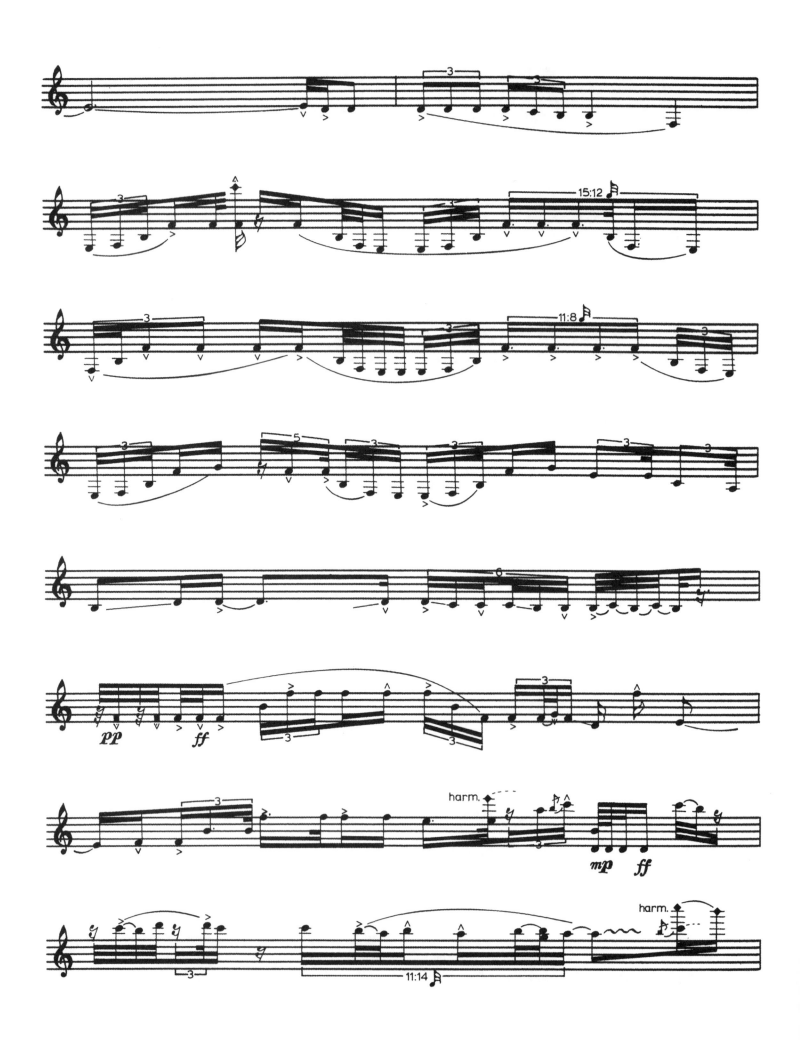

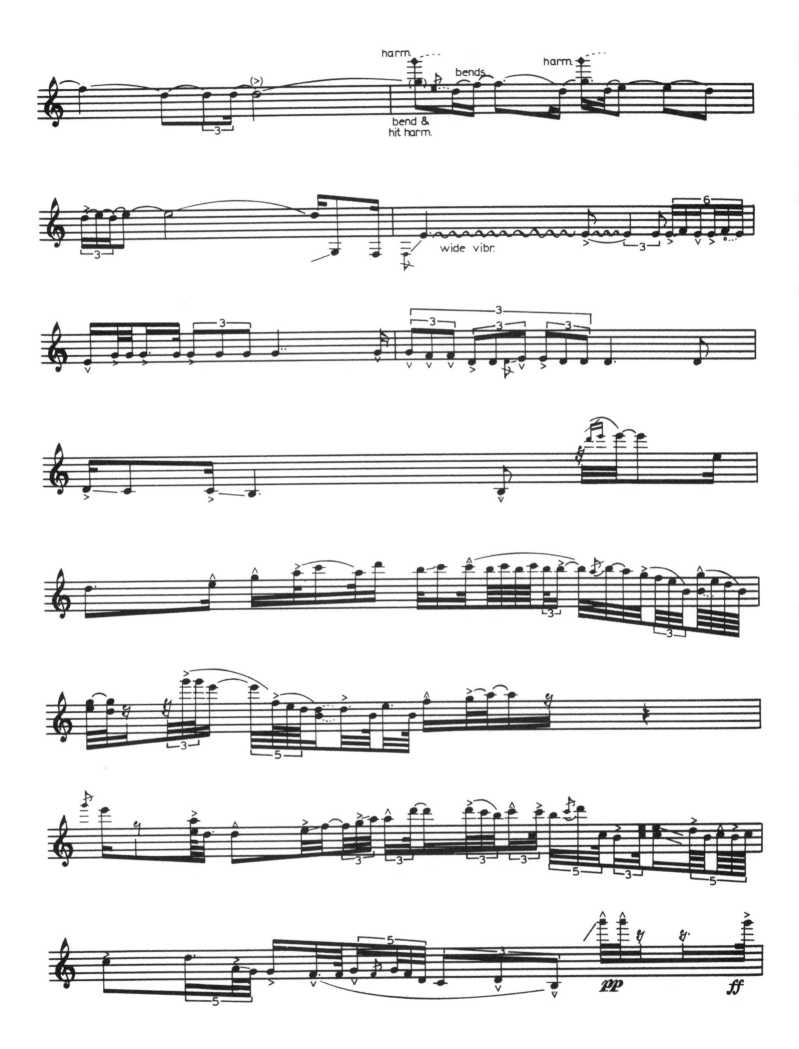

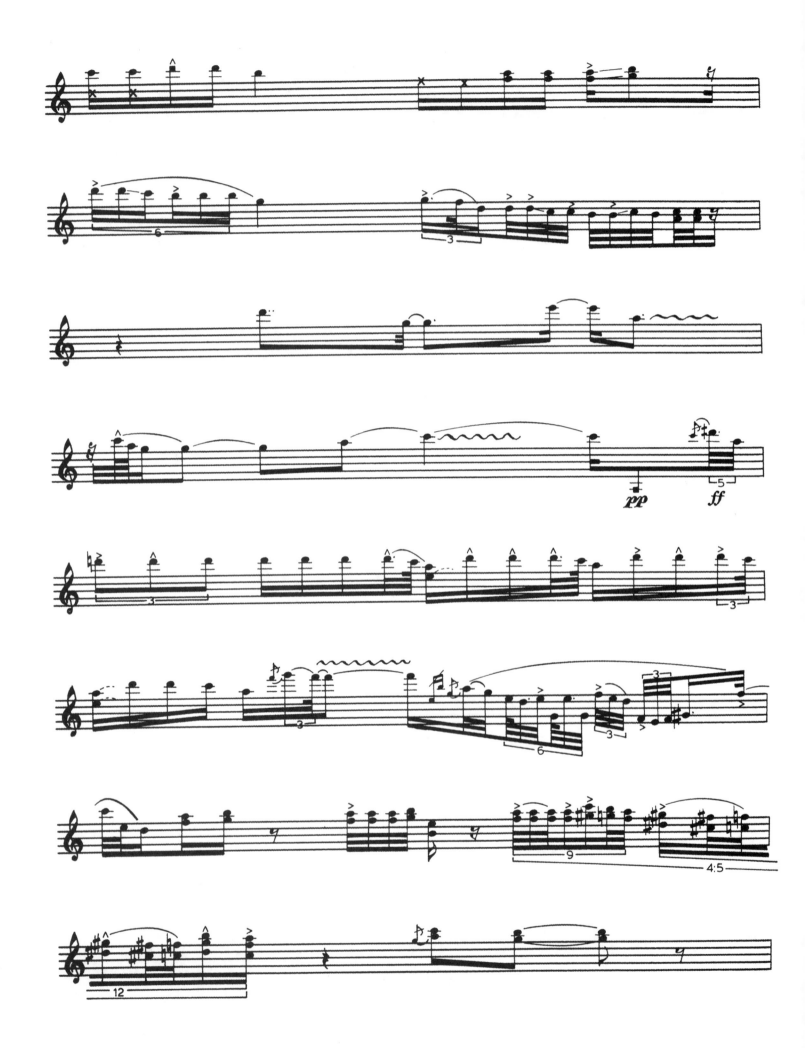

feed back spewage

SHUT UP'N PLAY YER GUITAR SOME MORE

Variations on The Carlos Santana Secret
    Chord Progression   108
Gee, I Like Your Pants   118
The Deathless Horsie   124
Shut Up 'n Play Yer Guitar
    Some More   136
        Vinny Colaiuta, drums
Pink Napkins   153

VARIATIONS ON THE CARLOS SANTANA SECRET CHORD PROGRESSION

Transcribed by
Steve Vai

by Frank Zappa

MEDIUM UP

on pick-up

111

GEE, I LIKE YOUR PANTS

Transcribed by
Steve Vai

by Frank Zappa

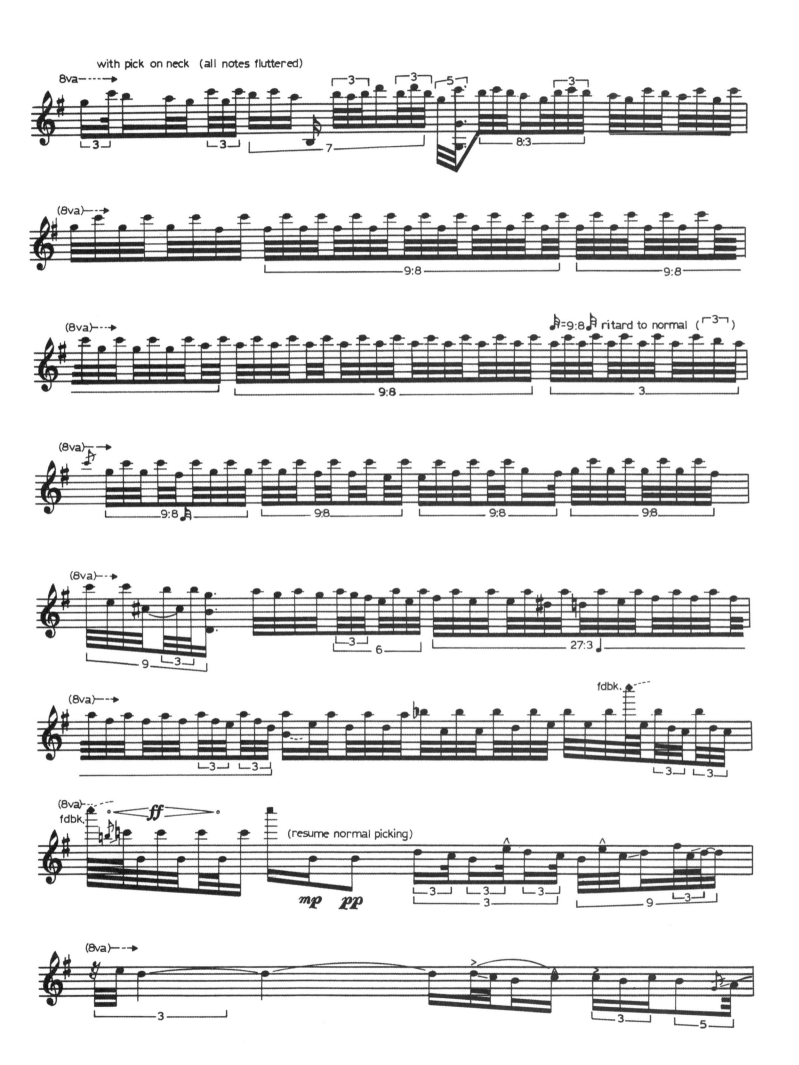

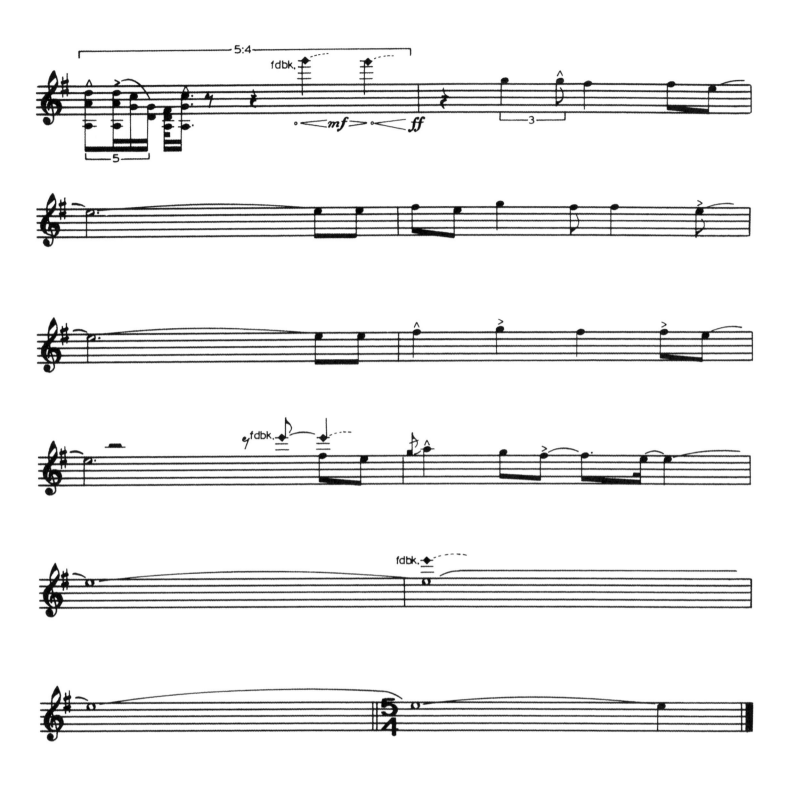

THE DEATHLESS HORSIE

Transcribed by
Steve Vai

by Frank Zappa

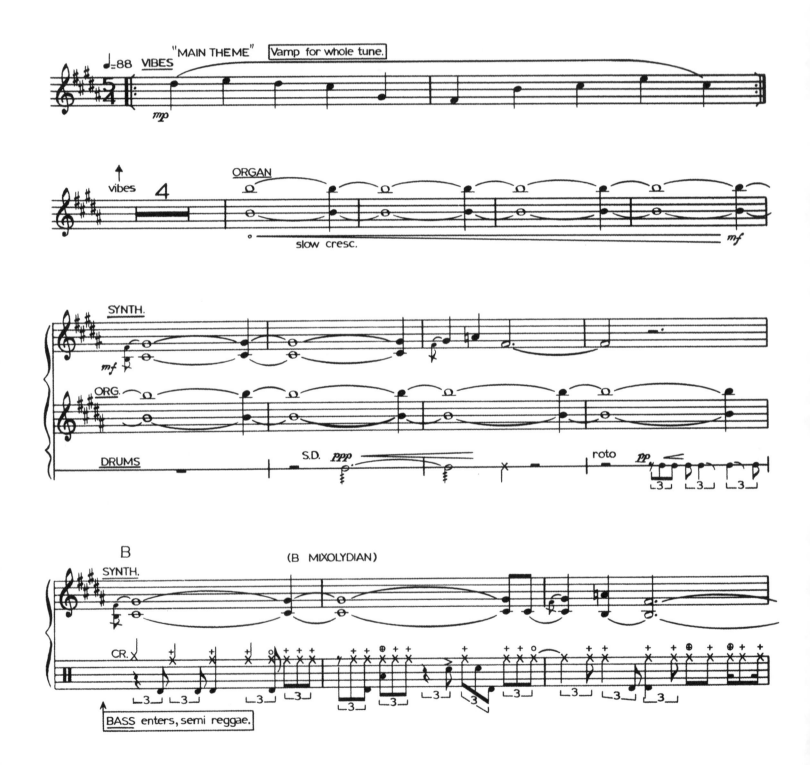

125

126

B pedal

135

SHUT UP 'n PLAY
YER GUITAR SOME MORE

Transcribed by
Steve Vai

by Frank Zappa

138

140

150

152

PINK NAPKINS

Transcribed by
Steve Vai

by Frank Zappa

154

RETURN OF THE SON OF SHUT UP'N PLAY YER GUITAR

Stucco Homes   160
Vinny Colaiuta, drums
Warren Cucurullo, rhythm guitar

Lead & Rhythm Guitars
and Drum Set

Guitars: tune E strings
to low D.

STUCCO HOMES

by Frank Zappa

Transcribed by
Steve Vai

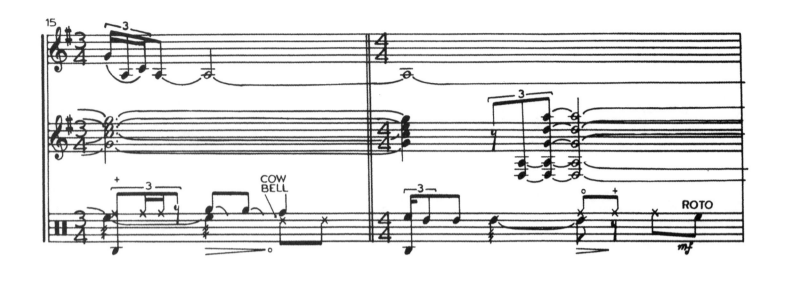

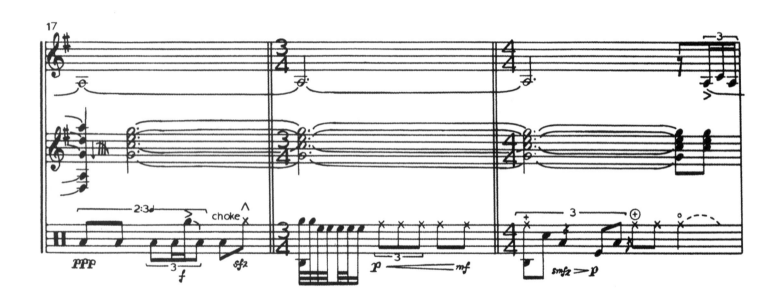

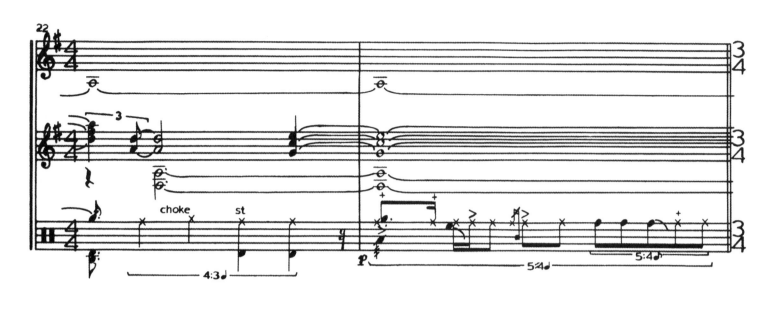

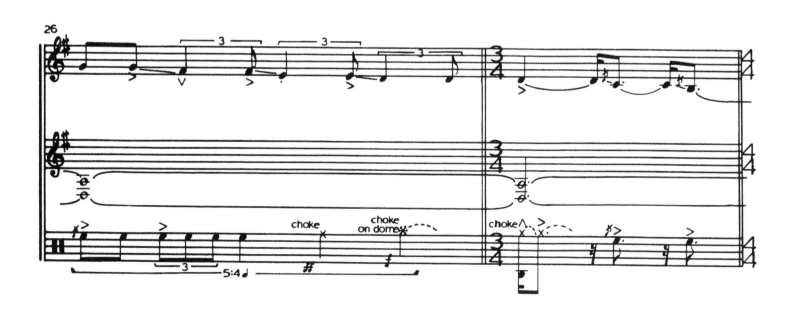

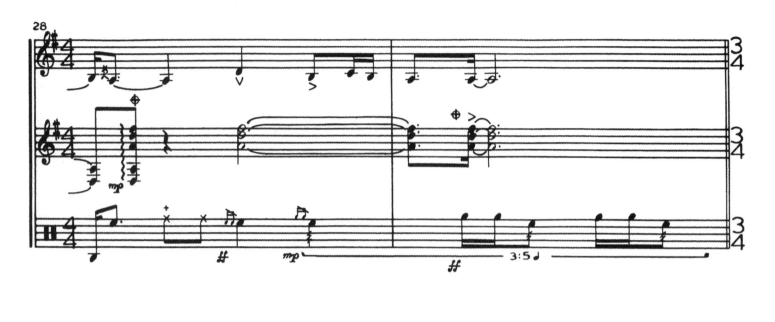

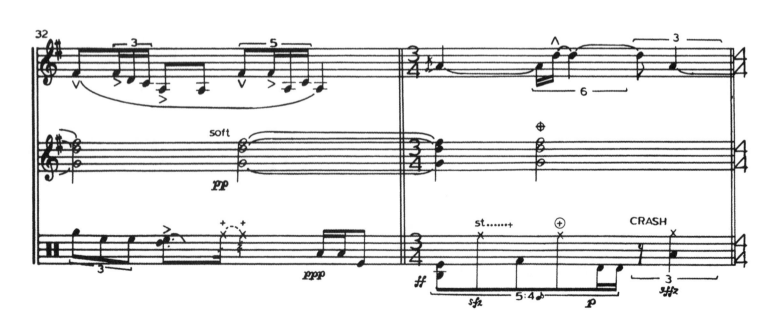

167

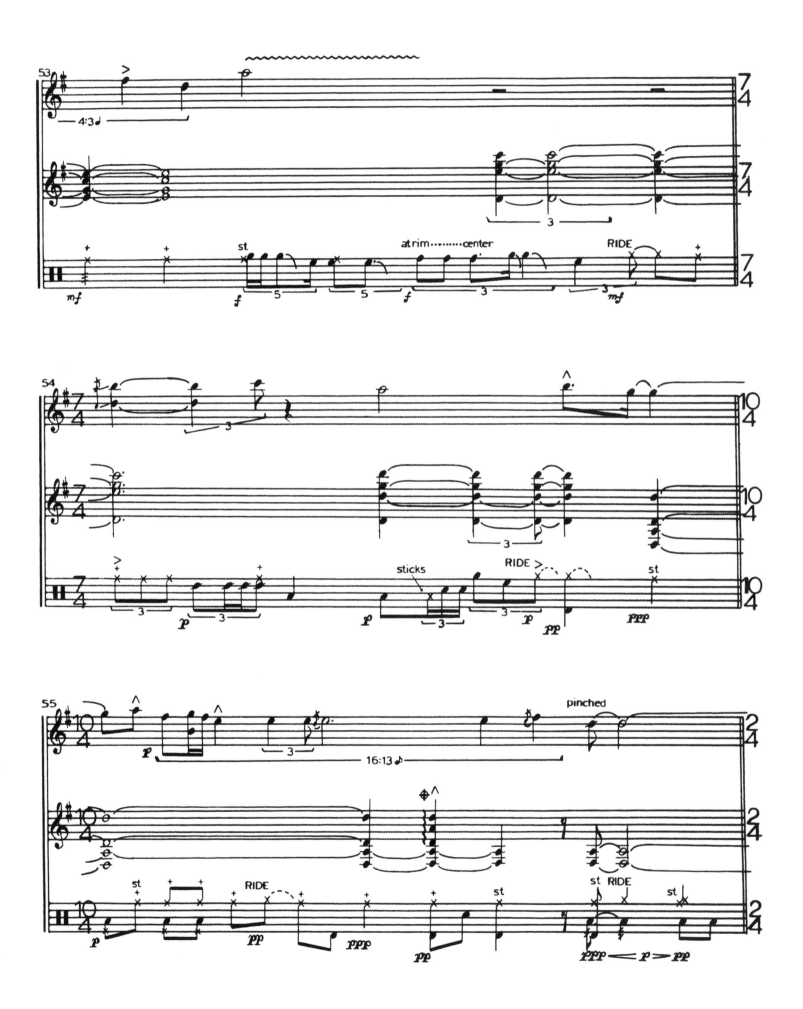

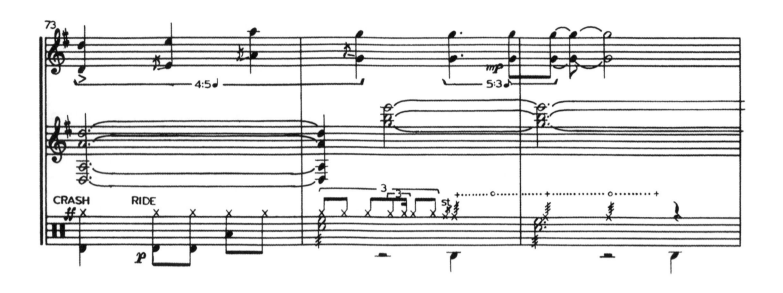

ARPEGIATE OCTAVES & MUTE STRINGS
with a "thumb strum"

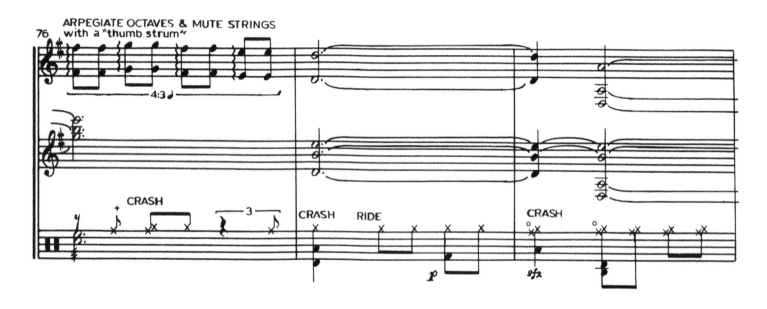

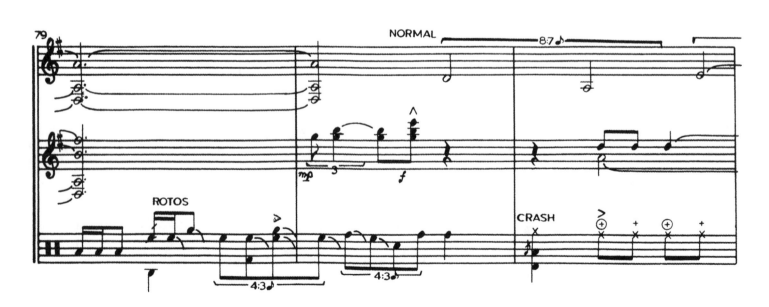

174

179

181

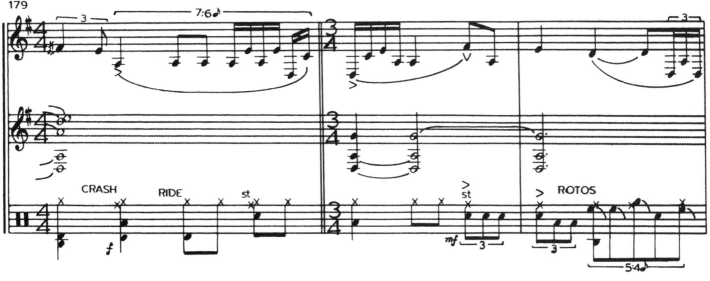

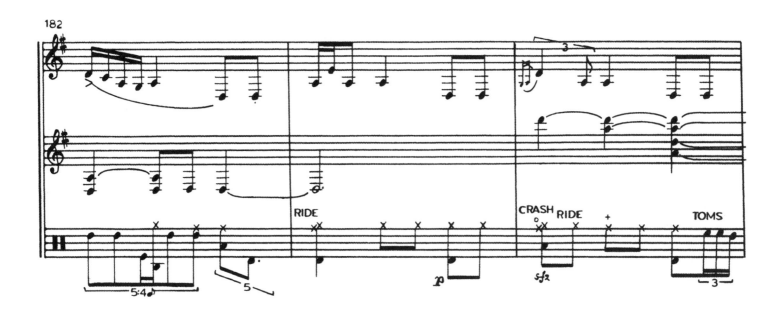

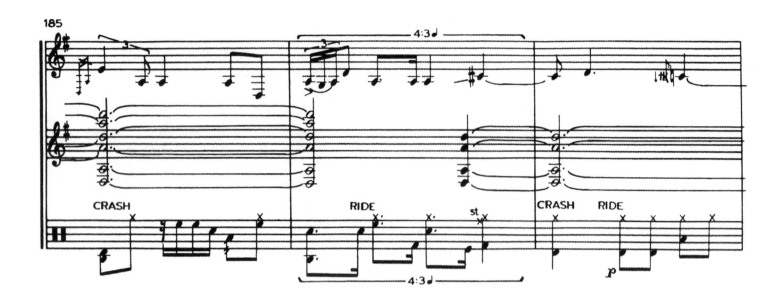

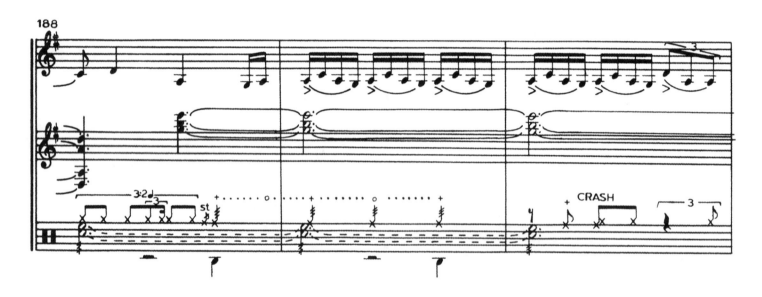

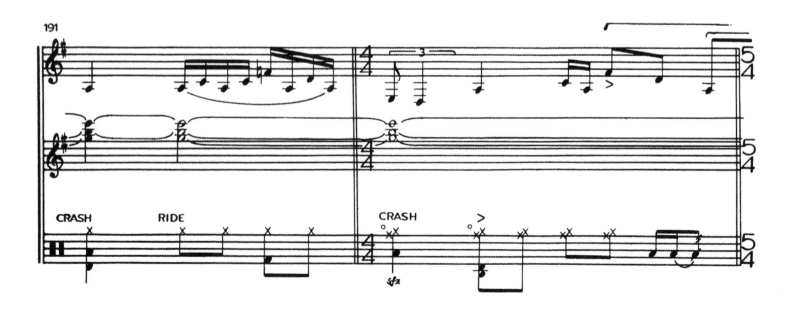

192

YOU ARE WHAT YOU IS

Theme from the 3rd movement of Sinister Footwear   206
Vinny Colaiuta, drums

Theme from the 3rd movement of
SINISTER FOOTWEAR

Transcribed by
Steve Vai

by Frank Zappa

207

Cluster of perc. instru-
ments: wd.blk.
c.b., castinets
etc.

add w.c.

w.c. out

JOE'S GARAGE ACTS II & III

Watermelon in Easter Hay 214
Packard Goose 226
Outside Now 243
He Used To Cut The Grass 250
    Vinny Colaiuta, drums

WATERMELON IN EASTER HAY

Transcribed by
Steve Vai

by Frank Zappa

215

RIDE
CRASH
H.H. step *sempre*

225

PACKARD GOOSE

Transcribed by
Steve Vai

by Frank Zappa

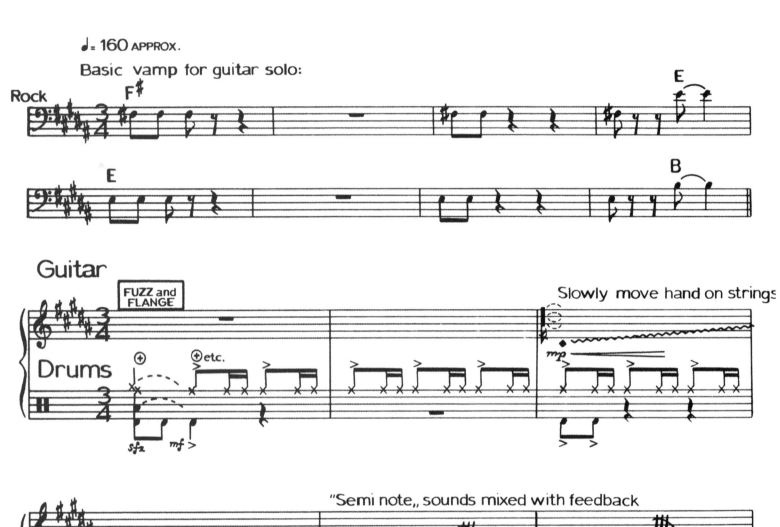

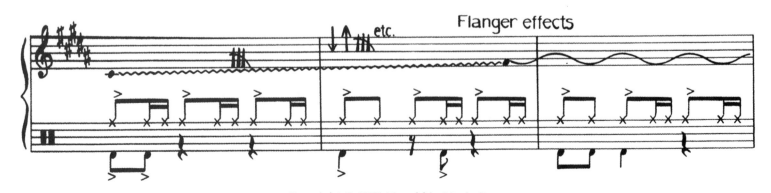

230

232

236

Drums

242

Guitar Solo
and Drums

OUTSIDE NOW

Transcribed by
Steve Vai

by Frank Zappa

244

246

HE USED TO CUT THE GRASS

Transcribed by
Steve Vai

by Frank Zappa

254

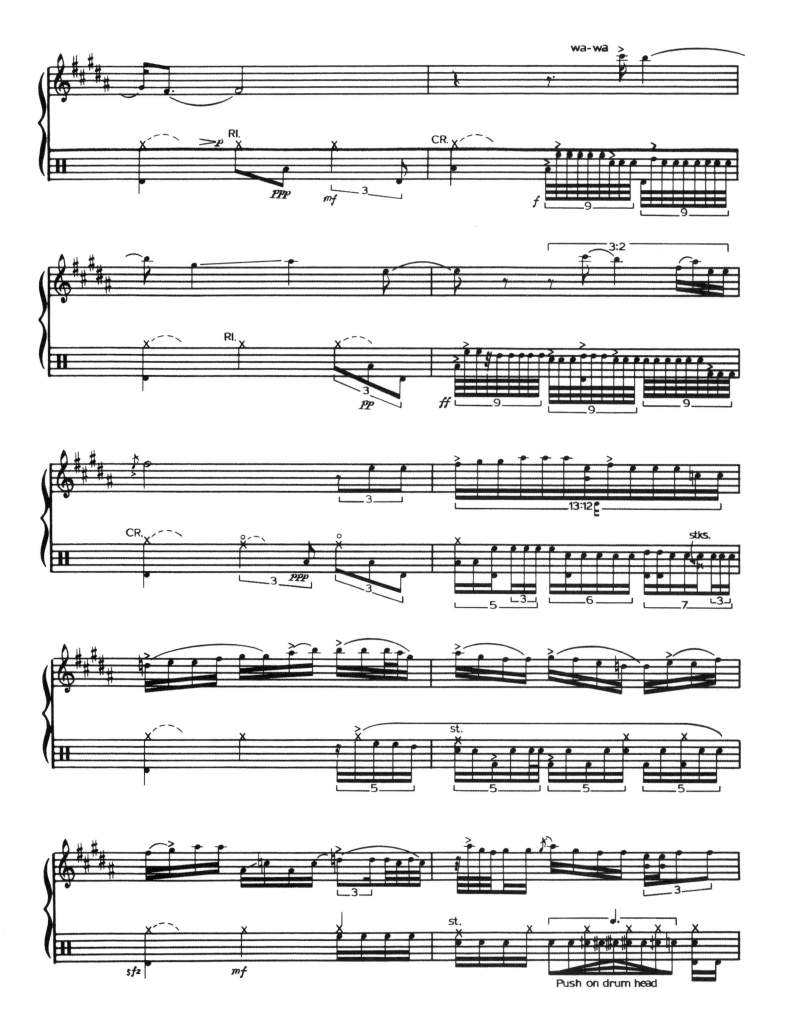

258

Mrs. Borg: *ff* (upset)

TURN IT

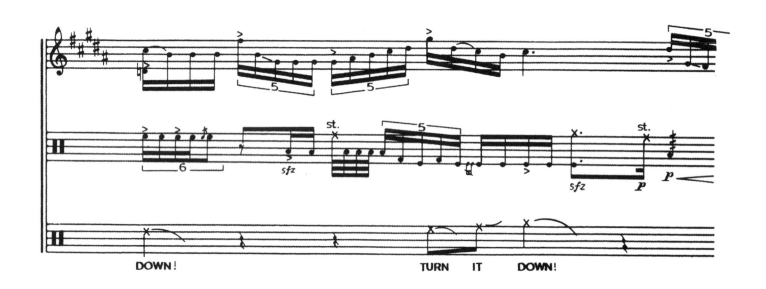

DOWN! TURN IT DOWN!

I HAVE CHIL - - DREN SLEEP-ING HERE

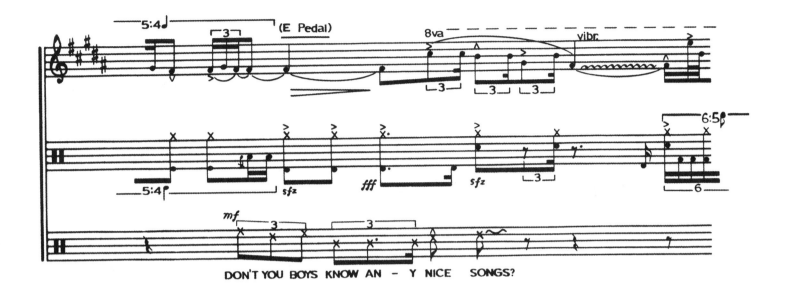

DON'T YOU BOYS KNOW AN - Y NICE SONGS?

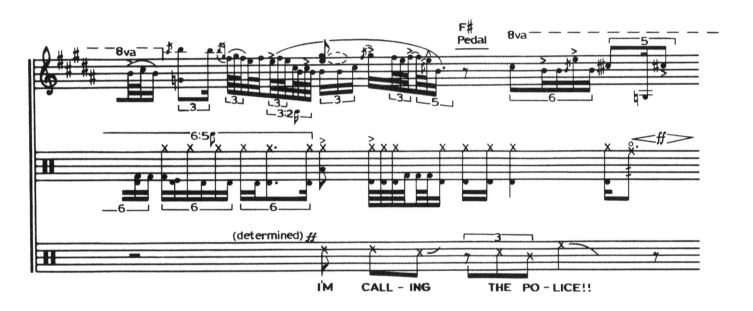

I'M CALL - ING THE PO - LICE!!

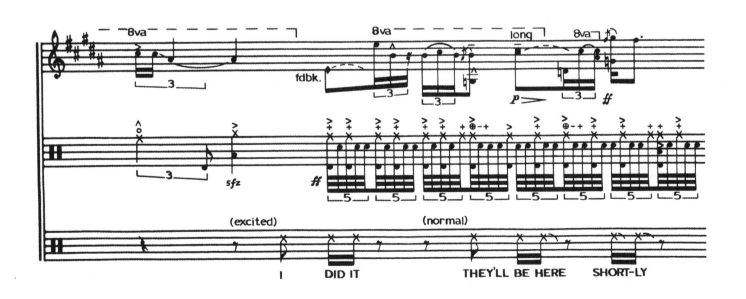

I DID IT THEY'LL BE HERE SHORT-LY

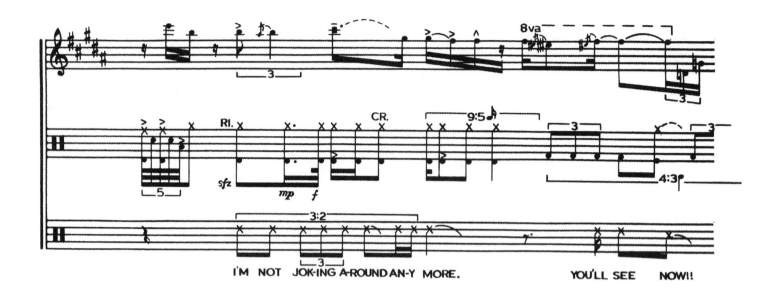

I'M NOT JOK-ING A-ROUND AN-Y MORE.   YOU'LL SEE   NOW!!

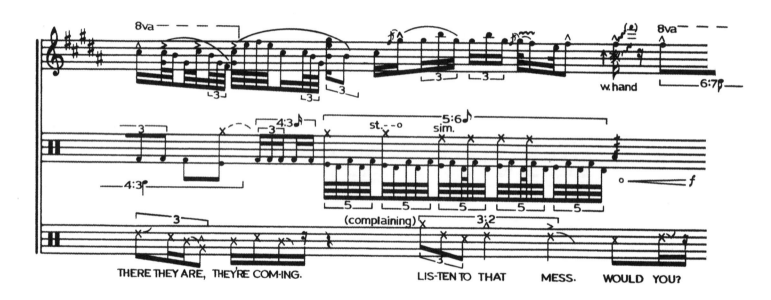

THERE THEY ARE, THEY'RE COM-ING.   LIS-TEN TO THAT   MESS.   WOULD YOU?

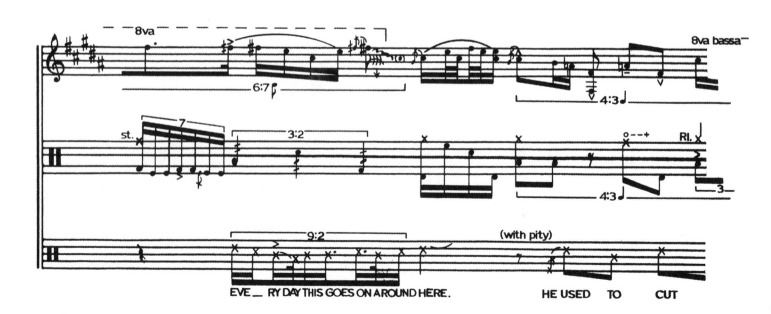

EVE __ RY DAY THIS GOES ON A-ROUND HERE.   HE USED   TO   CUT

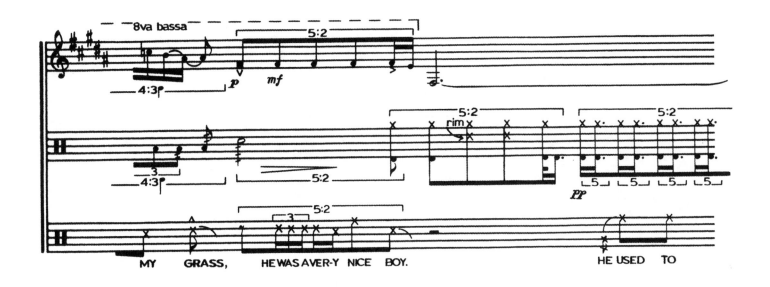

MY GRASS, HE WAS A VER-Y NICE BOY. HE USED TO

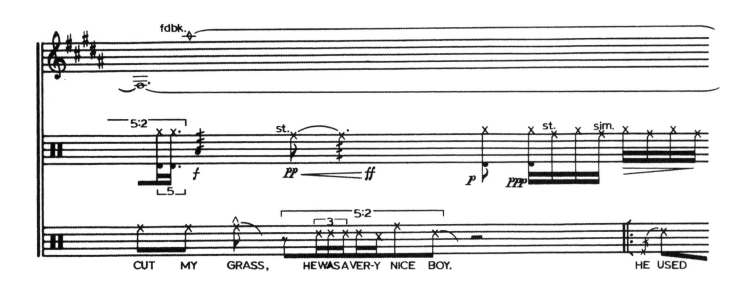

CUT MY GRASS, HE WAS A VER-Y NICE BOY. HE USED

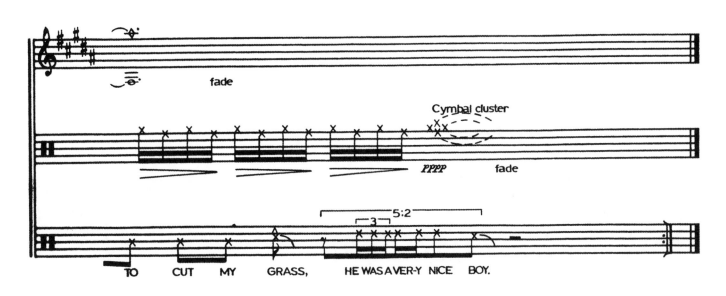

TO CUT MY GRASS, HE WAS A VER-Y NICE BOY.

SHEIK YERBOUTI

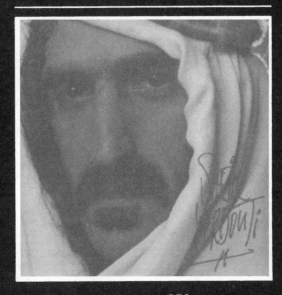

Sheik Yerbouti Tango   270
Rat Tomago   275
Mo' Mama   281
    Vinny Colaiuta, drums

SHEIK YERBOUTI TANGO

Transcribed by
Richard Emmet

by Frank Zappa

BASIC PULSE, NO BAR LINES

4

5:6

RAT TOMAGO

Transcribed by
Richard Emmet

by Frank Zappa

278

MO' MAMA

Transcribed by
Steve Vai

by Frank Zappa

287

ZOOT ALLURES

Black Napkins   292

BLACK NAPKINS

Transcribed by
Steve Vai

by Frank Zappa

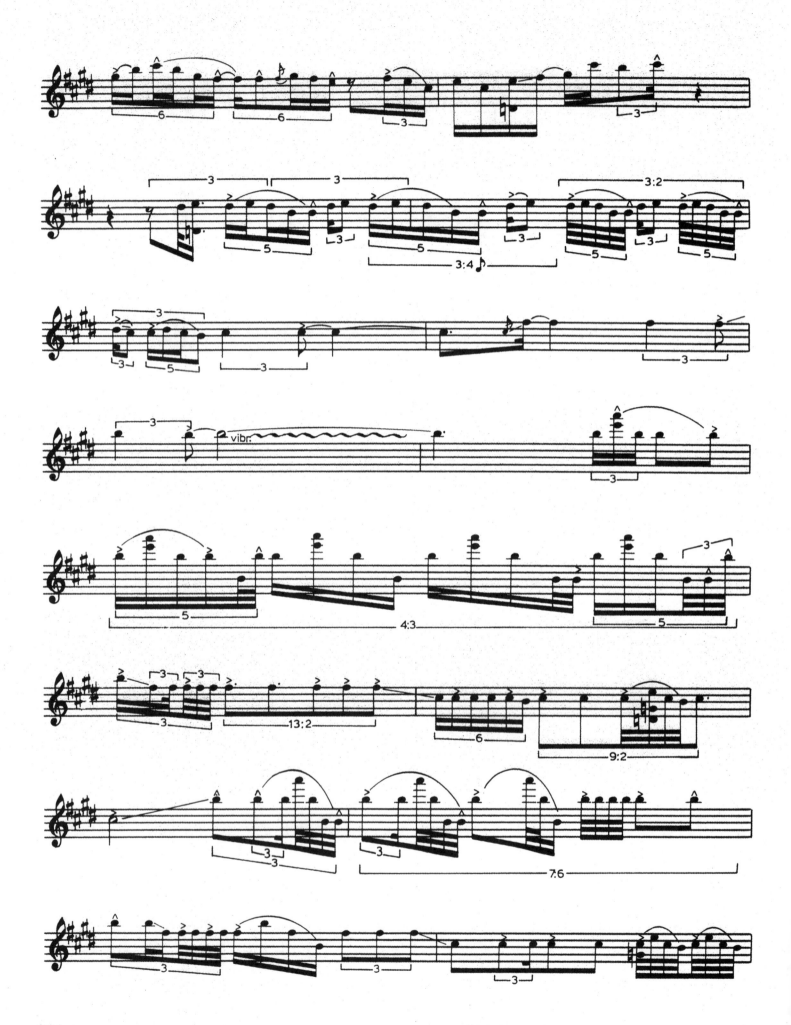

PULSE CONTINUES WITHOUT BARLINES

A FEW WORDS...

For Those Who Managed To Get This Far... by Frank Zappa

In preparing this book, we have tried to present the rhythmic and melodic events as exactly as possible (including my mistakes...*let's face it, some of those notes got played by a finger landing on the wrong fret or because I was rushing the tempo, or trying to catch up to a band that was running amok...*), and for the most part, I think we have succeeded.

If the notational results sometimes appear to be a little terrifying, you can console yourself with the thought that only a maniac would attempt to play these things anyway...*BUT,* if you should be a maniac sort of a person, *AND,* if you should try to read these charts on your own instrument, please be advised that if I were standing next to you with a metronome and a baton *(frowning and smoking a lot of cigarettes),* I would insist that the rhythms be accurate, and that only the pitches which reside outside the basic tonality *(the original "wrong notes")* could be altered.

We hope you enjoy this book, and we look forward to providing other study items like this in the future. Thank you for taking the time to read this.